GREAT CIVILIZATIONS

Ancient Rome

Longman

Contents

Top: The Temple of Vesta in the Forum. Centre: Mosaic of an antelope being loaded on to a ship, from a Roman house in Sicily. Bottom: Soldiers from Trajan's column, built to commemorate the emperor's victory over the Dacians.

Editorial

Author
Christopher Fagg B.A.

Editor
Abigail Frost M.A.

Illustrators
Nigel Chamberlain
Brian and Constance Dear

Cover
Richard Hook

LONGMAN GROUP LIMITED
*Longman House, Burnt Mill, Harlow, Essex CM20 2JE, England
and Associated companies throughout the world*

First published 1978
Second impression 1983

Designed and produced by Grisewood & Dempsey Ltd.,
Elsley House, 24–30 Great Titchfield Street,
London W.1.

Printed in Hong Kong by South China Printing Co.

BRITISH LIBRARY CATALOGUING IN PUBLICATION DATA
Fagg, Christopher
Ancient Rome. - (Great civilizations).
1. Rome – History – Juvenile literature
I. Title II. Series
937 DG213

ISBN 0 582 39003 6

NEAR EAST

EAST ASIA

The Ancient Romans

The Romans were a people of genius whose empire dominated the western world for 500 years. It was a patchwork of many different peoples. The Romans conquered the highly civilized Greeks of the east, and brought civilization to the wild Celtic tribes of the north and west. All were united under a single system of law. The Romans built their empire on a solid foundation of order, method, discipline – and courage. The *Pax Romana* – the Roman peace – brought prosperity and freedom to millions.

Rome and its empire fell at last to invading barbarian hordes. But Rome's influence lived on after the years of chaos that followed. When the troubled times were over the peoples of Europe built their new order on the Roman pattern – the only one they knew of. Slowly, over the centuries, their 'Roman' world has become the world we know today.

In this book we see how the Romans developed from a tribe of herdsmen in central Italy to become the rulers of an empire; we see how Rome's leaders governed their lands, and how ordinary Romans lived.

A Roman sacrifice. This circular relief is from the Arch of Constantine in Rome, built in AD 315. The relief itself, however, dates from much earlier.

The ruins of the Forum in Rome. It was the centre of life in the city, an open marketplace surrounded by temples and monuments: In the foreground, the remains of the Temple of Vesta: behind it, the arch of the emperor Titus.

Every city in the Roman empire had its public baths. They were more than simply a place to get clean – they were a centre for meeting friends and talking business. This beautifully decorated bathhouse is in Ephesus, Turkey.

The World of the Romans

'All roads lead to Rome' says the proverb. Rome at its greatest was indeed the centre of the western world.

The Roman empire was at its greatest during the 2nd century AD, when it joined together some 50 million people. It stretched from Britain in the north to the Sahara Desert in the south; from Spain in the west to Syria in the east. Its people all knew Latin, the Romans' language, and all were protected by the same system of law. Yet this great empire began as a small city-state in central Italy. Who were the Romans, and how did their empire come to be?

The first Romans were poor herdsmen who lived on the fertile plains of Latium in central Italy. Their city began as a collection of simple villages scattered on the hills which overlook the river Tiber. Between 700 and 600 BC the region was taken over by the Etruscans, a much more advanced people from the north. They rebuilt the villages of Latium as strong walled cities.

Rome became the most important city of the region. It was now ruled by kings, some of them Etruscan. But in 509 BC Roman nobles drove out their Etruscan king, whom they called Tarquin the Proud. The Romans hated the name of 'king' for ever afterwards. They were proud to say that Rome was governed by its Senate and People.

Over the next two centuries Rome grew in power. At last all of Italy was united under its leadership. Powerful foreign states feared that Rome might try to win an empire outside Italy. So they attacked it, hoping to halt its growth. But Rome and its Italian allies stood firm – and indeed won from one of its foreign enemies,

CHRONOLOGY

735 BC Legendary date of the founding of Rome.
509 Founding of the Republic.
494–493 Revolt of the Plebeians.
343–200 In a series of local wars, Rome emerges as the strongest power in central Italy.
281–275 First war with Carthage. Rome gains Sicily, Corsica, and Sardinia.
218–201 Second war with Carthage. Hannibal invades Italy. Romans defeat him and gain Spain.
214–167 Romans involved in wars in Greece and Macedonia.

133 Tribune Tiberius Gracchus is murdered after trying to introduce land reforms.
King of Pergamon bequeaths his kingdom to Rome.
123–101 Tiberius Gracchus's brother again proposes land reform but is killed.
83–79 Dictatorship of Sulla.
73–71 Slaves, led by Spartacus, revolt.
67 Pompey clears the Mediterranean of pirates.
59–51 Julius Caesar's wars in Gaul.
49 Caesar invades Italy and becomes dictator.
44 Caesar is assassinated.
44–31 Civil war between Mark Antony and Caesar's heir Octavian. Antony is defeated.
27 Octavian becomes 'first citizen' and is renamed Augustus.

14 AD Augustus dies. Tiberius becomes emperor.
37–41 Rule of Caligula, who proclaims himself a god. At last he is murdered, and his uncle Claudius, who has the support of the army, becomes emperor.
54–68 Reign of Nero. The last six years are marred by appalling cruelty. He kills himself after many plots and revolts.
69 Year of four emperors, all backed by different sections of the army.

69–96 The Flavian emperors. Under Vespasian, Titus, and Domitian the empire enjoys 25 years of stability.
96–192 The 'adopted emperors' – chosen for ability rather than family connections. This group includes the great Trajan and Hadrian.
193–235 The Severi – emperors from the family of Septimius Severus (193–211).
235–305 The 'soldier emperors'. A long period of attacks on the empire by enemies from all sides.

286–293 Emperor Diocletian divides the empire into four sections.
324–337 Civil wars; Constantine defeats his rivals and becomes sole emperor.
391 Christianity becomes the state religion of the empire.
395 The empire is finally divided into two parts, ruled from Rome and Constantinople.

404 The capital of the western empire moves from Rome to Ravenna. Italy is threatened by Goths and Germans.
410 Alaric the Goth sacks Rome.
476 Last western emperor is deposed.

Carthage, the islands of Sicily, Corsica, and Sardinia, and some land in Spain. These were the small beginnings of the greatest empire the western world had ever seen.

Power in Rome passed to the hands of one man, the emperor. At first this meant strong government, and peace. But there was always the problem of who was to take over when an emperor died. Above all, an emperor needed the support of the army – and at times different divisions of the army wanted different emperors. Moreover, as the empire grew it became difficult to defend and impossible for one man to govern. So at last the empire had to be divided. The western half – including Rome – soon fell.

After the fall

But Rome's influence did not die with its empire. The peoples of the provinces had learned many Roman ways. Many had become Christians. For them, Rome was still the centre of the world, for the Pope, leader of the Church, lived there. The Latin language lived on in such tongues as French, Spanish, and Italian.

Even today, we still have a great debt to Rome. Whenever a man is tried by a jury he may owe his freedom to a system invented by the Romans. Many Roman roads are still in use. The arch and the dome, which made all sorts of buildings possible for the first time, were spread through the empire by the Romans. Even the alphabet we use is the Roman alphabet. But the greatest debt of all is the idea that people of different nations can live together, united by common laws and ideals.

The Arch of Titus, who ruled briefly from AD 79 to 81. Even under the emperors, Rome was still supposedly governed by the Senate and People of Rome (Senatus Populusque Romanus) whose name appears on its inscription.

Empire at AD 14
added by AD 98
added by AD 116
Roads

York
BRITANNIA
London
GERMANIA
Paris
GAUL
Augsburg
RAETIA NORICUM
Bordeaux
Milan
PANNONIA
DACIA
HISPANIA
Massilia
Sirmium
ILLYRICUM
Lisbon
Caesaraugusta
ITALIA
MOESIA
Cordoba
ROME
THRACE
Pompeii
Byzantium
(Constantinople)
ARMENIA
MACEDONIA
CAPPADOCIA
ACHAEA
Sardis
MESOPOTAMIA
MAURETANIA
Athens
ASIA
Antioch
Carthage
LYCIA ET
PAMPHYLIA
SYRIA
NUMIDIA
Damascus
Timgad
JUDAEA
ARABIA
AFRICA
Leptis Magna
Cyrene
Alexandria
CYRENAICA
EGYPT

The Early Days

When the Romans founded their Republic, it was only one among many city-states. But in just three centuries it was the most powerful state in the Mediterranean.

According to Roman historians, the Roman Republic began in 509 BC. A group of Roman nobles – the Patricians – drove out the last king of Rome. The Patricians were the heads of the 100 leading families of Rome: their wealth and power came from the large estates they owned outside the city.

The Patricians lost no time in organizing the new state. In place of the king, they set two magistrates, called *consuls*. The consuls ruled the state and led the armies, but they had power only for one year. After the year was up, new consuls were elected. Below them were other, less powerful magistrates, such as the two *quaestors*, in charge of public finance. The magistrates were advised by a council, the Senate. Only Patricians were allowed to become magistrates or to be members of the Senate.

At first the Patricians ignored the rights of the common people, called the *Plebeians*. Then, in 490 BC, the Plebeians rebelled. Gathering on a small hill outside Rome, they elected their own leaders, the *tribunes*. They threatened to leave Rome and found their own city unless the Patricians gave them more rights. The Patricians, who needed Plebeian soldiers for the army, had to give in and recognize the tribunes.

The Plebeians had got their way by discussion rather than civil war. Slowly, they gained much more say in the way they were governed. They even won the right to enter the Senate and become magistrates. The greatest gain of all was a law passed in 287 BC. This said that the Assembly of the Plebeians, under the tribunes, could pass laws that were binding on the whole state.

Rome's power grows

The Romans had settled the quarrels between Senate and People not a moment too soon. The new republic faced rivalry from the many other city-states and peoples of Italy. For 250 years Rome was almost constantly at war. It made an alliance with the other cities of Latium against attacks by hill tribes, the Aequi and Volsci, and later against marauding Celts. There were wars with the Samnites, who were trying to take over the Greek colonies of Campania. But gradually the Romans made alliances with or conquered their neighbours until by 280 BC, all of central Italy was united under their leadership.

The Romans took great care not to

The symbol of Rome was the she-wolf who fed Romulus and Remus, the abandoned sons of the god Mars and a human princess, in the legend of its founding. When the boys grew up they set out to found a city, but they quarrelled and Remus was killed. So Romulus became the city's founder – and it was named Rome after him.

The Romans learned much from the Etruscans, who had wide contacts with the Greek world. This wall-painting, from an Etruscan tomb of the 6th century BC, shows a lively fishing expedition.

oppress the tribes and cities they controlled. They knew that harsh rule might lead to dangerous rebellions. Conquered peoples were offered special rights in return for military service. Nearby cities gained full Roman citizenship. Those farther away were allowed to govern themselves under the protection of Roman law. In areas where the Romans thought there might be trouble, they settled colonies of tough ex-soldiers. In time, these became towns.

Rome's growing strength attracted the attention of foreign enemies. In 280 BC a Greek king, Pyrrhus, brought a huge army to southern Italy. He was sure that Rome's allies would desert, giving him a great new empire. But the allies stayed loyal and, after a long struggle, Pyrrhus was forced to leave Italy. The cities of the south allied with Rome.

The next threat came from the Phoenician sea-traders of Carthage, who controlled the western Mediterranean from the coast of North Africa. Between 264 and 241 BC they fought and lost a bitter war with Rome for control of Sicily. Then in 218 BC, the Carthaginian general Hannibal led an army (and a number of war-elephants) from Spain and, crossing the Alps, ravaged Italy for 13 years. Despite a terrible defeat at

Cannae (216 BC), the Romans fought steadily in Spain, Italy, Sicily, and Africa. By 202 BC the power of Carthage was broken and its former empire was in Roman hands. These lands were the foundation of Rome's own empire.

Soon afterwards Rome was again at war, this time in the Greek-speaking east. The powerful rulers of Macedonia and Syria had joined together to menace Greece and Egypt. Roman armies, led by T. Quinctius Flaminius and the brothers Lucius Cornelius Scipio and Publius Cornelius Scipio, defeated both kings – but the trouble went on. In 148 BC the Romans made Macedonia into a province. Two years later, quarrels among the states of Greece led Rome to make Greece, too, a province. At the same time, a new revolt by Carthage was crushed and Carthage itself destroyed. By 133 BC, Rome controlled the Mediterranean world.

During all this time, it was the Senate which gave Rome the leadership it needed. In law, the People ruled Rome. But the Patricians of the Senate had the experience and ability that the People lacked. Patrician generals led Rome through the wars. The People were content to leave the state in the hands of the Senate.

Far left: War elephants were the 'tanks' of the ancient world. They were used by both Pyrrhus and Hannibal.

Above: The Appian Way, built as a supply-line for Roman forces during the Samnite Wars, in 312 BC.

A mounted Samnite warrior from Paestum, in southern Italy. The Samnites (Samnii) were a warlike Italian tribe with whom the Romans were often at war. They were finally conquered in 290.

Country Life

The nobles of the Republic were farmers. They looked forward to the times when they could leave the city and its politics for the quiet of the country.

The Romans were not just a city people. The farmers who lived in the surrounding countryside were also Roman citizens. For the first 400 years of the Republic, even the nobles who ruled Rome were first and foremost farmers. Country life in Italy changed only very slowly. There were three main kinds of farm: big estates, owned by the nobles; medium-sized farms; and smallholdings worked by a single peasant family. Near a town or city there would be vegetable gardens and orchards, pig and poultry farms.

The old-fashioned Roman noble was proud to live on his own estate. He would live in a large farmhouse, called a *villa*. All the other buildings a farmer would need were built on to the villa – sheds, granaries, a blacksmith's forge. Most of the work on an estate like this was done by slaves, but the Romans felt that a gentleman should, when needed, work beside his men in the fields. They had a proverb which said that the best fertilizer for any land was its master's eye. The villa's owner left his farm only for his public duties, such as serving in the

Above: A noble's tenants queue up to pay their rent – in kind. A basket of eggs, a rabbit, or some fish are equally acceptable to the landlord, who stands on the right.

An Italian villa in September. All the food needed by the owners and slaves is grown here; chickens and pigs are kept for meat, and goats for milk. There is also a vegetable garden. On the left men are harvesting grapes to be made into wine. Olives (for oil) and grain were also grown.

Senate or the army. He was glad to get back to it when his duties were over.

During the late Republic, things began to change. Citizens who had made money serving abroad returned to buy land with their new wealth. They built up huge estates and paid managers to run them, with slaves to do the work. Such a rich owner would live in a splendid house in Rome, and make very few visits to his estates. Small farmers found it hard to grow their crops as cheaply as these huge farms. Many peasants left the land and tried to find work in Rome. Often, they found only poverty.

Improving the land

The Romans were very interested in finding better ways of farming. Farmers could read books full of advice on how to match the right kind of crop to the

12

right kind of soil, or to make the land richer with manure.

The most important crop in Italy was grain. Wheat was grown for bread, and barley for animal food. The writers tell farmers to keep back the best of the crop to use as seed corn next year. Farmers experimented with different kinds of grain to find out which would give the best yield.

Just like farmers today, the Roman farmers changed their crops about, so that the soil would not lose its richness. A field where wheat had been grown one year would grow fodder crops – turnips, beans, or chick peas – the next. The bigger the farm, the greater the variety of crops that could be grown.

Wheat and barley can only be grown where the soil is good. Where the land was hilly and full of stones, farmers grew olives (used for making oil) and grapes (for wine) instead.

Most farmers had many animals – cattle, sheep, and goats. Close to towns and cities there were many smallholders who made a good living by raising chickens or pigs. Pork was a great delicacy. The most important of a farmer's animals were his oxen. They drew the plough and pulled the farm carts. They were the Roman farmer's 'tractor'.

FARM TOOLS

Roman farmers had many different tools to help them cultivate their land. The first job on a newly-settled piece of land was to break up hard ground with picks, mattocks, or a heavy two-pronged drag hoe. Then it was dug over with a long-handled spade or an ox-drawn plough. Light wooden ploughs with iron blades were best for light soil, or in hilly country. Where the soil was heavy clay, a bigger plough was used. It had an extra, knife-shaped, blade, called a coulter. The coulter was a Roman invention. It was mounted on the front of the plough and broke up heavy clods of earth which could then be turned over by the main blade.

A field had to be ploughed several times before the soil was fine enough for the seed to be sown. When it was ready a sower walked about the field scattering seed from a basket. Behind him came a plough to dig the seed in. Cereal crops – wheat and barley – were sown in the autumn.

At harvest time the farmer cut his cereal crops with a curved sickle. The crop was carried off to a stone threshing-floor, where it was usually trampled by horses to separate the grain from the straw.

A clay lamp, with a design of two men crushing grapes with their feet, to get the juice for wine-making.

The Republic Falls

Greed for the wealth of empire, and blindness to troubles at home, caused the Senate to become weak. The way was open for the rise of military dictators.

The last century of the Republic, from 133–30 BC, was a time of violence and civil war. These troubles were the result of a bitter struggle for power between the Senate and the Roman people.

What happened was that the Senate, which in the past had worked hard to make Rome strong and secure, had become selfish. Senators sent to govern the new provinces came back with huge fortunes made from taxing the inhabitants. Before, men had served Rome without any thought of gain. But suddenly, a career in politics became the pathway to vast riches.

A man who wanted to reach the top in Roman politics had to start by being elected to the post of *aedile*, or junior magistrate. From then on he could be elected to more and more important posts until he reached the highest office – that of consul. Only men who had been consul could be made governor of a province – and so get the chance to make a fortune.

The rich families of Rome used their money and influence to make sure that their own men got elected to the top posts. A man from outside this circle could only progress in his career by getting the support of a rich patron. In return, he was expected to vote the way his patron told him to.

A man who wanted to enter politics had to spend huge sums of money on bribing voters and on public shows such as games and circuses. An ambitious man like Julius Caesar had to borrow millions to pay for his career. Such a man *had* to get to the top – it was the only chance he had of paying back what he had borrowed.

The upper classes of Rome were so busy trying to make their fortunes that they became blind to the state of the people. Tribunes like Tiberius and Gaius Gracchus tried to force the Senate to grant public lands to poor farmers – many of whom were going out of business. But the big landowners of the Senate refused. They accused the tribunes of trying to overthrow the state and had them put to death. Roman politics split into two parties. The Populares backed the tribunes and the people against the Senate: the Optimates defended the powers of the Senate.

The age of the generals

Rome was weakened by the struggle between the parties at home at the very time it faced grave dangers abroad. There were revolts in Africa and the east, while in the north the new province of southern Gaul was menaced by barbarian tribes. In Italy itself, Rome's allies rebelled against harsh treatment, and there was also a revolt of slaves led by an ex-gladiator, Spartacus.

Gaius Julius Caesar (102– 44 BC).

THE DEATH OF THE REPUBLIC

On the 15th of March, 44 BC, Julius Caesar was stabbed to death in the Forum. His murderers were a group of senators led by Cassius and Brutus. Almost immediately, Rome was plunged into 14 years of civil war. Caesar had always been popular with the people, and his murderers, instead of being hailed as the saviours of the Republic, were forced to flee. Mark Antony was left in control — but not for long. Caesar had left a fortune in his will to his nephew Octavian, who now returned from abroad. Octavian persuaded his uncle's troops to join him. With their backing, he forced Antony to give him a share of the government.

Soon afterwards, Antony went to the east to do battle with Parthian invaders. While there, he made an alliance with Cleopatra, the queen of Egypt. It became clear that Antony and Cleopatra were planning to take over Rome's eastern empire and rule it themselves. Octavian denounced Antony as a traitor and declared war on Egypt. In 32 BC, his fleet met that of Antony and Cleopatra at the battle of Actium, off the coast of Greece. Octavian was the victor.

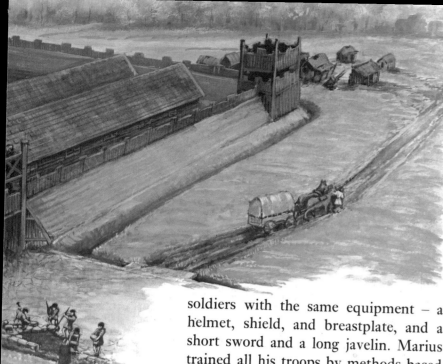

Far right: Reliefs from Trajan's Column, showing some of the activities of Roman soldiers.

The Roman legionary was a well disciplined, highly trained foot-soldier. He wore a metal helmet, shoulder guards, body armour, and shin guards. As time went on, more and more of the troops guarding the frontiers were non-Italians from the provinces.

soldiers with the same equipment – a helmet, shield, and breastplate, and a short sword and a long javelin. Marius trained all his troops by methods based on those used in the gladiator schools. Marius's army was divided into many legions – rather like modern regiments. Each legion was divided into ten cohorts of 600 men and each cohort into six centuries – units of 100 men.

A strong officer class was in control of this efficient army. The consul was the supreme commander. Under him there were six military tribunes, and 60 centurions for each legion. Each centurion commanded a century. Discipline was tough. The centurion's badge of office was the vine-staff with which he beat his men.

The army of the empire
But the army that Marius had made to defend the Republic in the end helped to destroy it. Men who fought for pay were more likely to be loyal to the generals who paid them than to the state. Sulla, Pompey, Julius Caesar, and Augustus all ruled because of the loyalty of their armies – not because they had been elected to power. Augustus realized this.

Augustus needed to build an army which could defend the frontiers, but remain completely loyal to the state and its leader. First he disbanded the huge armies left over from the civil war. He cut the army down to 28 legions, and

In this desperate time, the Romans were lucky to find great generals like Marius, Sulla, Pompey, and Caesar. The problem was that these men were not simply army commanders. They were ambitious politicians who thought even more of their own glory than the good of Rome. They defeated Rome's enemies and then marched back to Rome with their armies and demanded their reward.

Marius and Sulla were on opposite sides. Marius was a *novus homo* (new man), a man from outside the top Roman families. He was elected consul six times with the backing of the Populares. Sulla, on the other hand, was an Optimate who backed the Senate. They clashed when the Senate appointed Sulla to lead an army to the east to defeat the rebel king Mithridates. Marius was furious at not being sent himself. He waited until Sulla had left, then descended on Rome with an army. He and his supporters began a reign of terror, slaughtering huge numbers of Optimates. He had himself made consul, but died shortly afterwards. When Sulla got back from the East, he found Rome in the hands of the Populares. He marched his army up from the south and captured the city. There was a new wave of executions – but this time it was the Populares who suffered. For three years Sulla ruled Rome as dictator: he crushed the powers of the People and made the Senate stronger. Then he retired.

It was not long before Rome was once again torn by civil war. The consul Pompey, a general who had defeated

Caesar refused. Instead, he invaded Italy. In two years he defeated Pompey's armies in Greece, Egypt, Asia, and Spain. Caesar was now master of Rome.

Caesar ruled with a firm hand. He made sure that the Senate would do what he wanted by trebling its number of members. The new senators were men who owed their place to Caesar. Caesar knew that they would be loyal to him. But he still had enemies. Some senators were afraid that Caesar might try to make himself a king. They hatched a plot to murder him.

Civil war followed Caesar's death. His second-in-command, Mark Antony, quickly dealt with the murderers. But the wars were not over. A bitter dispute arose between Antony and Octavian, Caesar's heir, for control of the empire. The defeated Antony killed himself.

Spartacus and conquered vast new lands in the east, gave the People back all the powers that Sulla had taken away. Pompey planned to rule Rome with his allies, Crassus and Caesar. Both Pompey and Caesar became consuls, although the Senate opposed them. In 59 BC Caesar was given the province of Gaul, which was under pressure from northern Celts and Germanic barbarians. In eight years Caesar conquered all France.

Pompey began to be afraid of Caesar's power. In 49 BC he ordered Caesar to disband his army and return to Rome.

Politicians of the late Republic bought votes by putting on lavish public shows. Above: a wild beast show, depicted on a coin of about 42 BC. Lions, tigers, leopards, elephants, even polar bears were brought to Rome to be hunted to death in the arena. Often, criminals were condemned to be torn apart by wild beasts for the sport of the watchers. Left: A chariot race in the Circus Maximus, shown in relief on a moulded clay lamp. Four quadrigae, four-horse chariots, race for the turning post before a packed crowd. Below left: Terracotta figurines of gladiators. They wear heavy helmets with tall crests: their legs are protected by greaves.

Voting scene from a coin, 106 BC. One man puts his token in a voting box, while another receives his voting tablet.

Rome'

The discipline of
work in peace he

Roman army regulation
dictated that even a
temporary encampment
should be solid and we
defended. Each soldier
carried an entrenching
tool with which to dig a
defensive ditch. The ea
was thrown up to make
rampart, covered with
turf, and set with a stou
fence of stakes. Inside,
men and their
commanders lived in
leather tents. More
permanent camps, like t
one in Dacia, were built
the same square pattern
but with wooden or ever
stone buildings. All camp
had special areas set
aside for stabling,
baggage, kitchens, and s
on: as far as possible,
these areas would be in
the same position in ever
Roman camp.

A stone garrison building
built in Timgad (Algeria),
in the first century AD.

The First Citizen

Augustus is listed as Rome's first emperor. But he preferred to be known as the 'First Citizen'.

With Antony dead, the long years of bitter civil war were at an end. Octavian swiftly set about the task of rebuilding the state. The first thing that he did was to lay aside the special powers he had held during the war. He re-started the yearly elections. He himself stood for the post of consul and was elected.

The Romans were grateful to the man who had brought them peace. They loaded him with honours and gave him the title Augustus – meaning 'Revered One'. They were ready to grant him anything he asked. If he had wanted to, he could have been a dictator – but this was not Augustus's way. Instead he brought back the ways of government of the Republic. This made him still more popular. But he was careful to keep control of the army in his hands.

There was much to do. At home, Augustus set to work to improve the system of government. He reformed the Senate, getting rid of unworthy senators, and fining those who were too lazy to go

to its meetings. At the same time, he began to reorganize the empire.

His chief problem was the border to the north where Germanic tribes threatened to invade Italy. Augustus sent his generals Agrippa, Drusus, and Tiberius to drive the tribes back. His generals conquered huge new territories. In this way, Augustus made a ring of provinces to defend Italy from barbarian tribes. The new frontier ran along the rivers Rhine and Danube.

Augustus then turned to the business of governing the empire. He appointed paid governors from the ranks of the senators, and tried hard to make sure that they governed fairly. Above all, he made it easier for provinces to appeal to Rome if suffering bad government.

In order to make certain that his orders were carried out, Augustus had to develop his own civil service. His household slaves and freedmen handled a stream of letters to and from his headquarters in Rome. To speed up contact with distant provinces, Augustus set up a postal service – the *cursus publicus*. His messengers could travel 80 kilometres (50 miles) in a day, staying the night at special way-stations.

In Rome, Augustus lived simply and treated his fellow-citizens as equals. Despite his great power, he listened respectfully to the advice of the Senate and was careful to follow the laws. He worked hard to bring back the old-fashioned Roman virtues – respect for the gods, hard work, and duty. He rebuilt temples and passed laws to make people observe the feasts of the gods.

Augustus wanted to make Rome a city worthy to govern an empire. He spent vast sums of his own money on new public buildings, employing the best architects and sculptors of the day. He gathered around him a group of artists, writers, and poets – including Virgil, whose long poem, the *Aeneid*, glorified the history of Rome.

Far left: The 'Gemma Augusta', a carved gem portrait of Augustus. It shows him as an ideal ruler in the Greek manner – heroic, strong, and wise.

Members of the Praetorian Guard. Augustus formed this hand-picked troop to be the emperor's personal guard and to control Italy. Later, the Praetorian Guard became a powerful voice in choosing new emperors.

The highest point

Between AD 69 and [...] empire reached its hig[...] the most part it was gov[...] emperors. They worked [...] frontiers safe. Vespasia[...] luxury and waste in R[...] appointed a brilliant go[...] to bring peace to the rel[...] of Britain. Trajan, bor[...] Spain, led his armi[...] barbarians on the D[...] Later, he conquered [...] Romania) before, in AD [...] expedition against the[...]

Right: One of the most magni[...] seen in Rome was an emperor[...] prisoners and plunder from su[...] were paraded through the stre[...] carved on the triumphal Arch [...] carry spoils from the Temple [...] Titus's suppression of the Jev[...] Left: This statue of the empe[...] him not as the modest and po[...] but as a living image of the m[...] tramples underfoot a woman, [...] conquered province. Below: [...] Hadrian's villa at Tibur (mod[...]

The Empire

The many different nations that made up the empire were united under the emperor. The emperors were as different from one another as their provinces.

The Roman empire grew up over a very long time. The first overseas province, Sicily, was gained in 227 BC. The last two provinces, Dacia and Arabia, were added in AD 106 – three centuries later.

The Romans hardly ever went to war simply for love of conquest. They gained their empire, piece by piece, because they needed a ring of states between their enemies and their homeland. Macedonia and Greece became a buffer between Italy and the powerful kingdoms of the Near East. These in turn were conquered when their rulers caused too much trouble for Rome. In the north the frontiers were pushed to the Rhine and Danube rivers in order to keep barbarian tribes away from the northern boundaries of Italy.

As the empire grew, so the Romans had to find a way to govern their provinces. During the Republic, the Senate chose magistrates (called at first *praetors*, later *proconsuls*) from its own ranks, and sent them abroad to govern for a year. But this system worked very badly. Even a good governor could not learn enough about his province in such a short time. On the other hand, there were many bad governors who treated their year of office as a chance to squeeze as much money as possible out of the inhabitants.

Augustus realized that this must change. In the provinces under his control he appointed paid governors (*legati*). He was the first ruler to keep firm control over how the empire was governed. Gradually, the running of the

empire came to be completely in the hands of one man – the emperor.

The frontiers of the empire were guarded by the army. From Augustus onwards, the emperors were careful to keep the army as small and as far away from Rome as possible. The legions were stationed in permanent camps. These were linked by a network of roads so that forces could be switched from one place to another as they were needed. In time, the camps became centres of trade and towns grew up around them.

The empire grows up

Slowly, Roman civilization spread across the marshes and forests of western

The southern limit of the Roman empire was the North African desert. Today, the desert has crept into what were once fertile farmlands. The wealthy Roman town of Leptis Magna in Libya now stands surrounded by dry sand.

The empire's northern edge was the frontier between Britannia and the wild lands of Caledonia. The frontier was fixed by Hadrian with a great wall running between the Solway Firth and the river Tyne.

Europe. New tow[n]
and the conquere[d]
like Romans. U[nder]
brought under
engineers drained
the rivers and buil[t]
The servants of t[he]
kilometres (50 mi[les]
orders to the pr[o]
towns and cities a[nd]
people elected the[ir]
their affairs. Only
difficult to settle
Rome for a decisi[on]

In fact, the pro[vinces relied]
less and less on R[ome]
became important
also made for th[ings]
as glass, pottery,
had once import[ed]
still had a vast i[n]
tribute paid by th[e]
rest of Italy trade[d]
because it was ch[eaper]
and food from th[e]
or grow them in [Italy]

Nero, the emperor who ruled so badly that at last he had to flee from Rome. He was more interested in music and the arts than in ruling justly, and the Romans rose up against his cruelty.

Below: How Augustus reorganized the empire. Peaceful provinces were governed by the Senate; newer provinces were governed by the emperor. Client kingdoms were ruled by their own kings, who accepted Roman authority.

The emperors
Even towards the
he had all the p[ower]
Augustus was
meaning 'leading
least Rome was
Romans had beco[me used to]
being led by one [man]

Senatorial provinces
Imperial provinces
Conquests of Augustus
Client states

A small metal figure of a slave cleaning a boot.

The houses of wealthy Romans were richly decorated with wall-paintings. This one, showing a garden, comes from the palace of Livia, the wife of the emperor Augustus. Gardens were a popular subject for these paintings; they give the impression that the solid walls of the house have melted away to reveal trees and flowers. After a day spent in the bustle of Roman public life, such a feeling would have been a welcome relief.

Belo[w]
tom[b]
Rom[an]
His
tear
husb[and]

Belo[w]
Pomp[eii]
at wo[rk]
work
men
piling
goods
stree[t]
lived
above
wood[en]

Many of the people of Rome and its empire were slaves. Many of them had come to Rome after being captured in wars abroad. They were sold, and the profits went to the state to help pay for the war. Once sold, a slave became the personal property of his owner — just like the owner's house or furniture. A son would inherit his father's slaves.

The Romans did not use slaves simply to do heavy, unpleasant work. A slave might work as a full-time household servant, serving meals and looking after the children. Or he might act as his master's secretary and look after his business affairs. Some rich men ran large workshops staffed entirely by slave craftsmen. These were the nearest thing the Romans knew to a modern factory. Great landowners relied on slaves to work on their country estates. Most families could afford only one or two household slaves. But some rich men owned hundreds.

Officially, Roman law treated slaves very harshly. For a long time, there were no limits set on how badly a master might treat his slaves. All a slave might hope for was a kind master. Some men took a great interest in their slaves, paying for their education and lending them money to start them in business. Many slaves were able to save enough to buy their freedom, and many others were *manumitted* (freed by their masters without having to pay anything).

common people. He was expected to know the name of everyone (rich or poor) that he met while walking in the street or the forum. In later years politicians had special slaves to whisper the names of people they met into their ears!

A rich man rose at daybreak and gathered his household together for family prayers. Then, after a light breakfast of bread, cheese, and wine, it was time for him to see his *clientes*. These were men who called on rich citizens to offer their services. In return they hoped for political favours, or simply a gift of money or food.

After this, the citizen called his steward – a male slave – to write down his orders. There might be business to do with his country estate, or an invitation for the slave to deal with. Then the citizen set off for the law-courts or the Senate. These were crowded and noisy; after a long morning, the citizen must have been glad of a visit to the baths during the hottest part of the day. Here he could meet his friends.

The evening meal was taken early – usually no later than 4 o'clock. Romans often gave dinner parties for their friends. Six or seven guests was thought the best number. The host, his wife, and their guests ate their food reclining on elegant couches. It was rare for a meal to continue long after dark.